The Art of
WEALTH CREATION

A Beginner's Guide for Financial Success

VIJAYKUMAR KRISHNAMOORTHY

Managing Director & CEO
Ricchie Rich Investments

ISBN
Paperback 979-8-89777-939-0
Hardcase 979-8-89961-845-1

ABOUT RICCHIE RICH INVESTMENTS

Ricchie Rich Investments Pvt Ltd, established by Mr. Vijaykumar Krishnamoorthy, Managing Director & CEO, has been successfully serving clients for several decades. Our expertise lies in goal-oriented financial planning. As an AMFI-registered mutual fund distributor and financial product distributor, we go beyond offering generic mutual fund recommendations. Instead, we provide personalized suggestions tailored to your unique financial goals and risk appetite.

At Ricchie Rich Investments, we follow a holistic approach to financial planning. We collaborate with clients to develop customized goal sheets and execute transactions accordingly.

Our commitment extends beyond transactions we strive to build lasting relationships. As part of our journey together, we provide continuous support through regular portfolio reviews, indepth analysis, and seamless execution of purchase and redemption transactions, ensuring you stay on track to achieve your financial goals.

With an efficient back-office team and highly experienced professionals, we ensure a smooth and hassle-free investment experience. Clients receive monthly reports, timely updates, and access to user-friendly apps to track their portfolios effortlessly.

If you are looking for comprehensive, goal-driven investment planning and personalized investment recommendations, feel free to reach out to Ricchie Rich Investments.

DISCLAIMER

The content, plans, data, and illustrations presented in this book are based on personal experience and knowledge. They are intended solely for informational and educational purposes and should not be considered as financial advice. Before making any investment decisions or acting on the information provided in this book, it is highly advisable to consult a or Qualified Financial Advisor or a AMFI registered Mutual Fund Distributor.

Mutual fund investments are subject to market risks. The return figures mentioned in this book are based on past performance and should not be interpreted as a guarantee of future results. Before investing, it is crucial to carefully review scheme-related documents and conduct thorough due diligence.

Financial markets and investment instruments can be complex, with their performance influenced by numerous factors. Seeking expert advice and conducting proper research are essential steps in making well-informed financial decisions. This book aims to provide knowledge and insights, but it should complement, not replace, professional financial guidance.

The author, publisher, and any parties involved in the creation and distribution of this book bear no responsibility for investment decisions made by readers without consulting financial professionals. It is strongly recommended that you take the time to understand the complexities of the investment options available and approach the financial concepts in this book with caution and prudence.

This book by Ricchie Rich Investments is for educational purposes only. Its content may not be reproduced, distributed, or used commercially . It does not constitute financial, investment, or legal advice. Ricchie Rich Investments is not responsible for any actions based on this content.

ACKNOWLEDGMENTS

I take great pleasure in acknowledging the dedicated collaborative efforts of Mahalakshmi. B and Keerthivasan. B in bringing this book on the fundamentals of mutual funds to life. Their expertise, meticulous research, and commitment to delivering valuable financial knowledge have been instrumental in shaping this resource.

This book has been designed to serve as a comprehensive yet accessible guide for individuals seeking to understand and navigate the world of mutual funds. Through their combined efforts, have ensured that complex concepts are simplified, making this book a practical tool for both beginners and aspiring investors.

I extend our sincere gratitude to them for their invaluable contributions, which have helped create a resource that will empower readers with financial awareness about Mutual Funds.

Table of Contents

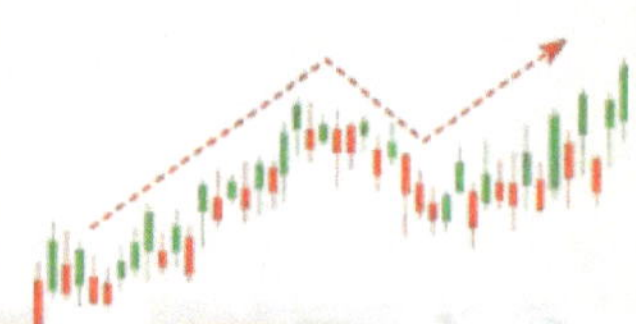

Table of Contents

What is Mutual Fund?

A mutual fund aggregates capital from multiple investors to construct a professionally managed portfolio comprising equities, fixed-income instruments, or other securities. It grants individual investors exposure to diversified asset allocations tailored to distinct investment strategies and return objectives. However, mutual funds impose annual management fees, expense ratios, and commission charges, which can impact overall returns.

Why invest in Mutual Fund?

A layperson often lacks the expertise to invest in the stock market. Mutual Funds (MF) enable individuals to benefit from higher returns by pooling funds from investors, creating a corpus, and investing in equities (shares) and debt instruments (debentures) of reputed, high-rated companies. Professional fund managers with expertise and experience handle these investments.

Benefits of Mutual Fund

1. Diversification

Mutual funds spread investments across various asset classes like stocks, bonds, and other securities, reducing the risk of loss. Even if one asset underperforms, others may balance it out, ensuring better stability.

2. Professional Management

Managed by experienced and qualified fund managers who analyze market trends, monitor performance, and make informed investment decisions on behalf of investors.

Equity mutual funds are the perfect solution for people who want to own stocks without doing their own research.

3. Affordability

Mutual funds are accessible to all investors, enabling them to begin with modest sums through Systematic Investment Plans (SIPs), starting at just ₹250 per month.

– PETER LYNCH

4. Flexibility

A variety of schemes are available to match different goals growth funds for long-term wealth, income funds for regular returns . Investors can choose funds based on their risk tolerance and objectives.

5. Liquidity

Open-ended mutual funds allow investors to buy or sell their units at any time, making it easy to access funds when needed. However, tax saving funds like ELSS have a lock-in period.

6. Transparency

Fund houses provide regular updates through fact sheets, monthly reports, and portfolio disclosures, helping investors stay informed about their investments' performance.

7. Tax Benefits

Investments in Equity-Linked Savings Schemes (ELSS) qualify for tax deductions of up to 1.5 lakhs under Section 80C (Income Tax Act). Additionally, ELSS presents the opportunity for substantial returns, subject to a mandatory lock-in period of three years.

"I made my first investment at age eleven I was wasting my life up until then"

– WARREN BUFFETT

Operational Framework of Mutual Fund

Mutual funds pool investor money, allowing for professional management and diversification. Fund managers invest in a variety of securities, and the fund's performance determines the returns earned by investors.

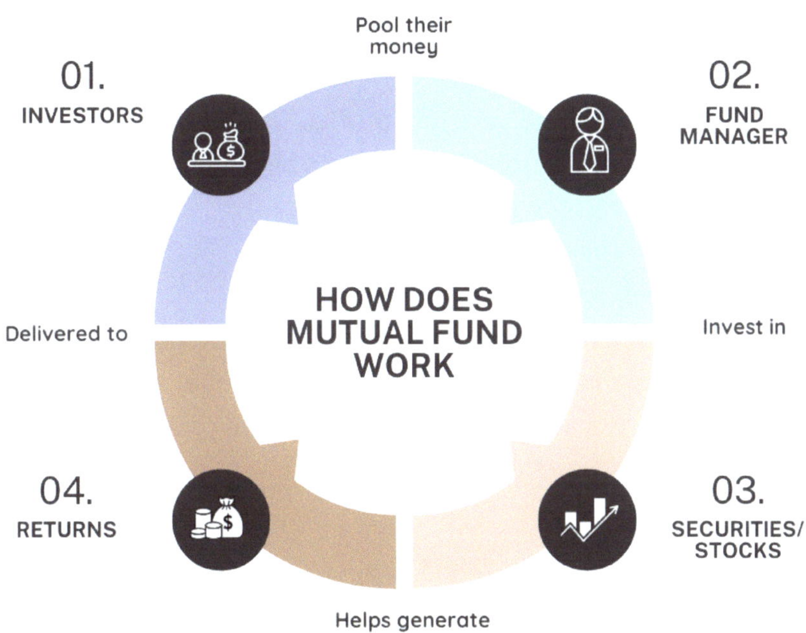

✓ Investors Pool Their Money:
Multiple investors contribute varying amounts of money to a central fund. This pooling of resources allows for diversification and access to investments that might be out of reach for individual investors.

✓ Fund Manager:
A professional fund manager is responsible for managing the pooled money. Their expertise is used to invest the funds in a diversified portfolio of stocks, bonds, or other securities.

✓ Investment in Stocks/Securities:
The fund manager carefully selects and invests the pooled money in various securities, such as stocks and bonds. This diversification aims to spread risk and potentially generate higher returns.

✓ Returns Generation:
Through the fund manager's investment decisions, the mutual fund aims to generate profits. These profits are then distributed among the investors based on their initial investment and the fund's performance.

✓ Returns Delivered to Investors:
The returns generated by the mutual fund are distributed to the investors in the form of dividends or capital appreciation. These returns can be reinvested in the fund or withdrawn by the investors.

"The big money is not in the buying and selling, but in the waiting."

– CHARLIE MUNGER

Key Players in the Mutual Fund Industry

A mutual fund operates through a structured framework of entities, each ensuring efficient management, investor protection, and compliance with regulations.

Asset Management Company (AMC) – The Fund Manager Firm

The AMC is the company that manages the mutual fund and makes investment decisions on behalf of investors. It is responsible for creating, managing, and administering mutual fund schemes.

Key Functions of an AMC:

- ✓ Designing mutual fund schemes based on investor needs (e.g., equity, debt, hybrid funds).

- ✓ Collecting money from investors and investing it in financial instruments like stocks, bonds, etc.

- ✓ Managing the fund's portfolio to achieve the investment objectives.

- ✓ Ensuring compliance with regulatory guidelines set by SEBI.

EXAMPLE

HDFC Asset Management Company manages various mutual fund schemes under the HDFC Mutual Fund brand.

Fund managers are professionals employed by the AMC to manage specific mutual fund schemes. They are responsible for making investment decisions such as which stocks, bonds, or other securities to buy or sell.

Key Responsibilities of Investment Experts:

✓ Conducting market research and analysis to identify profitable investment opportunities.

✓ Aligning the fund's portfolio with its investment objectives (e.g., growth, income).

✓ Managing risks associated with market fluctuations.

✓ Monitoring the fund's performance regularly and making necessary adjustments.

EXAMPLE

A fund manager for an equity mutual fund will focus on investing in stocks with high growth potential.

Trustees are independent individuals or entities responsible for ensuring that the mutual fund operates in the best interests of investors. They are appointed by the AMC but work independently to supervise its activities.

Key Responsibilities of Trustees:

- ✓ Ensuring that the AMC follows SEBI regulations and the mutual fund's objectives.

- ✓ Monitoring the AMC's operations to safeguard investor interests.

- ✓ Reviewing the performance of the AMC and ensuring that investors are not misled or harmed.

- ✓ Approving key decisions, such as changes in the fundamental attributes of a mutual fund scheme, to protect investors' rights.

EXAMPLE

If an AMC proposes a major change in a scheme's investment strategy, trustees must review and approve it to safeguard investors' rights.

A custodian is a financial institution that holds the securities in which the mutual fund invests. It ensures that the fund's assets are stored safely and are not misused.

Key Responsibilities of Custodians:

✓ Holding and safeguarding the securities (e.g., stocks, bonds) purchased by the mutual fund.

✓ Settling transactions when the fund buys or sells securities.

✓ Providing regular reports on the fund's holdings and transactions.

✓ Monitoring compliance with investment limits and regulations to protect investor interests.

EXAMPLE

If a mutual fund invests in stocks, the custodian will hold those stocks in the fund's account to ensure they are not lost or stolen.

Regulatory Bodies – SEBI (Securities and Exchange Board of India)

In India, SEBI regulates mutual funds to ensure transparency, investor protection, and compliance with the law. It sets the rules and guidelines for AMCs, trustees, custodians, and other participants.

Key Responsibilities of SEBI:

- ✓ Registering and approving new mutual fund schemes.

- ✓ Ensuring that mutual funds disclose all necessary information to investors.

- ✓ Monitoring the performance and operations of AMCs to prevent fraud.

- ✓ Protecting investors by enforcing rules on fees, disclosures, and risk management.

EXAMPLE

SEBI mandates that mutual funds must clearly disclose the risk level of each scheme, helping investors make informed decisions.

How These Participants Work Together

Investors put their money into a mutual fund scheme. The AMC manages the fund, with fund managers making investment decisions.

Trustees oversee the AMC's operations to protect investors. Custodians safeguard the assets purchased by the fund. SEBI ensures that all participants follow the rules and maintain transparency.

Classification of Mutual Fund

Mutual fund schemes can be classified into different categories based on structure, investment objectives, asset class, and special features.

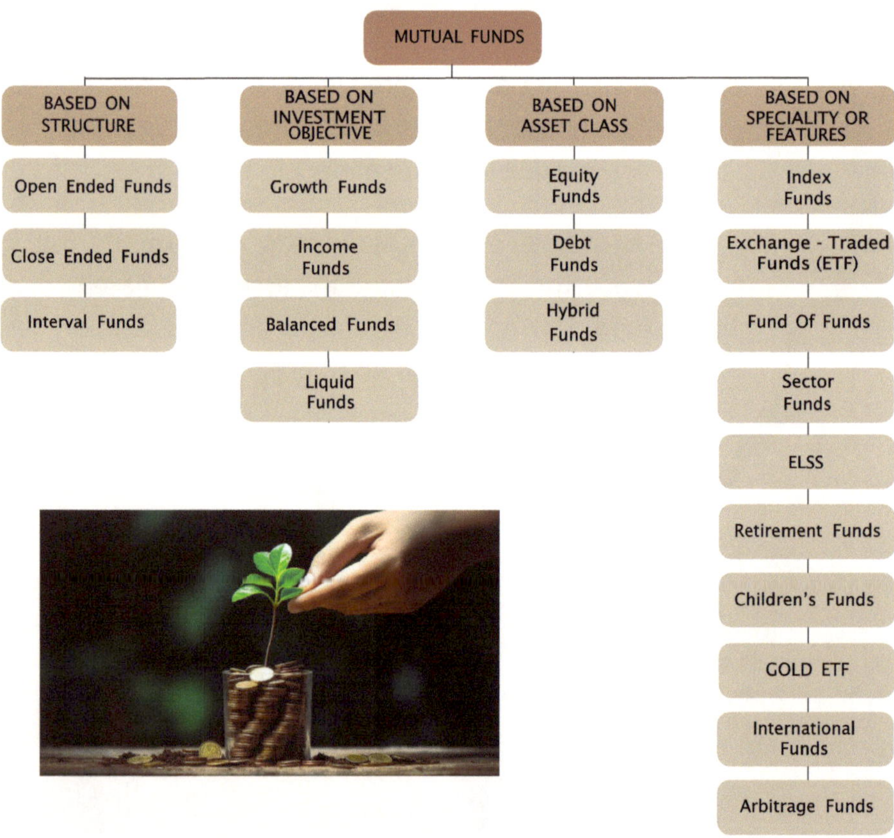

Open-Ended Funds

Open-ended mutual funds do not have a fixed maturity period. Investors can buy or sell units at any time based on the prevailing Net Asset Value (NAV).

Key Features:

Liquidity: High

Flexibility: Investors can enter or exit anytime

Suitable For: Investors seeking flexibility and liquidity

Close-Ended Funds

These funds have a fixed maturity period. Investors can subscribe only during the New Fund Offer (NFO) period, and after that, the fund units are traded on stock exchanges.

Key Features:

Lock-in period: Typically 3-5 years

Liquidity: Limited (can be traded on stock exchanges)

Suitable For: Investors willing to stay invested for the long term

"An investment in knowledge pays the best interest."

A hybrid between open-ended and close-ended funds. These funds open for transactions at specific intervals.

Key Features:

- ✓ Redemption: Allowed only during specified intervals

- ✓ Suitable For: Investors looking for a balance between liquidity and stability

DID YOU KNOW........

Mutual fund industry's AUM surges over 500% in a decade. Indian mutual fund industry's assets under management (AUM) saw significant growth over the last decade, as it increased by a whopping 524 per cent to 68.08 lakh crore in November 2024 from 10.9 lakh crore in November 2014.

Rural and semi-urban areas now account for 50 percent of the total SIP accounts in the country. Meanwhile, AUM growth in B-30 (Beyond 30 cities) outpaced the top-30 cities during this period.

Growth Funds

- Objective: Focus on capital appreciation by investing primarily in equity stocks.
- Risk Level: High
- Suitable For: Investors with a high-risk appetite and long-term investment horizon

Income Funds

- Objective: Focus on generating regular income by investing in debt securities like bonds, debentures, and government securities.
- Risk Level: Moderate
- Suitable For: Conservative investors looking for stable returns

Balanced Funds (Hybrid Funds)

- Objective: Aim to balance risk and return by investing in a mix of equity and debt instruments.
- Risk Level: Moderate to High
- Suitable For: Investors seeking both growth and stability

Liquid Funds

- Objective: Focus on providing liquidity and low- risk returns by investing in short-term debt instruments like Treasury Bills and Certificates of Deposit.
- Risk Level: Low Suitable
- For: Investors looking for short-term investment options with low risk

EQUITY FUNDS

- Invest primarily in equity shares of companies.
- Risk Level: High
- Suitable For: Investors with a long-term investment horizon

Equity Fund Category	Minimum Investment	Description
Large Cap Fund	At least 80% in large-cap stocks	Focuses primarily on companies with large market capitalizations
Large & Mid Cap Fund	At least 35% in large-cap stocks and 35% in mid-cap stocks	Balanced exposure to both large and mid-sized companies
Mid Cap Fund	At least 65% in mid-cap stocks	Focuses on mid-sized companies with growth potential
Small Cap Fund	At least 65% in small-cap stocks	Targets smaller companies with high growth prospects
Dividend Yield Fund	Predominantly invest in dividend yielding stocks, with at least 65% in stocks	Focuses on companies that consistently pay high dividends

Equity Fund Category	Minimum Investment	Description
Value Fund	Value investment strategy, with at least 65% in stocks	Follows a value investment strategy by investing in undervalued stock
Focused Fund	Focused on the number of stocks (maximum 30) with at least 65% in equity & equity related instruments	Concentrates on a limited number of stocks (maximum 30) for better returns
Multicap Fund	At least 25% in Large, Mid and Small cap	Investment spread across large, Mid and Small cap Stocks.
Sectoral/ Thematic Fund	At least 80% investment in stocks of a particular sector/ theme	Invests in a specific sector or theme, like IT, pharma, or ESG
Contra Fund	Scheme follows contrarian investment strategy with at least 65% in stocks	Adopts a contrarian approach by investing in out-of-favor stocks with potential turnaround opportunities

DEBT FUNDS

- Invest in fixed-income securities such as bonds, debentures, and government securities.
- Risk Level: Low to Moderate
- Suitable For: Conservative investors seeking stable returns

Debt Fund Category	Investment Focus	Description
Money Market Fund	Highly liquid instruments like T-bills and commercial papers with maturities < 1 year	Lowest risk and return; suitable for short-term parking of surplus funds
Overnight Fund	Securities maturing overnight	Highly liquid with very low risk; ideal for parking funds for 1-day duration
Liquid Fund	Securities with maturities up to 91 days	Slightly higher risk and return than Overnight Funds; suitable for short term needs
Ultra Short Duration Fund	Securities with maturities up to 6 months	Slightly higher risk and return compared to Liquid Funds
Low Duration Fund	Securities with maturities up to 1 year	Higher risk and return than Ultra Short Duration Funds

Debt Fund Category	Investment Focus	Description
Short Duration Fund	Securities with maturities between 1 to 3 years	Moderate risk and return; suitable for medium-term investments
Medium Duration Fund	Securities with maturities between 3 to 7 years	Higher risk and return compared to Short Duration Funds
Medium to Long Duration Fund	Securities with maturities between 7 to 10 years	Higher risk and return than Medium Duration Funds
Long Duration Fund	Securities with maturities greater than 10 years	Highest risk and return among duration-based funds

💡 *Myth: Mutual funds are only meant for long-term investments to earn higher returns.*

☑ *Fact: Equity mutual funds are great for long-term returns*

🔲 *, but other types of mutual funds can help you achieve short- term, medium-term, and long-term goals too* 🕐 🎯

✦ *There's a mutual fund for every timeline and goal* 💰 ✳

HYBRID FUNDS

- Invest in a mix of equity, debt, and other asset classes to balance risk and return.

- Risk Level: Moderate to High

- Suitable For: Investors seeking both growth and stability

Hybrid Fund Category	Minimum Investment	Description
Aggressive Hybrid Fund	Minimum 65% to 80%	Focuses on higher equity allocation for significant capital appreciation; involves higher risk
Arbitrage Fund	Minimum 65% in equity	Exploits price differences between cash and derivatives markets; generally low-risk with moderate returns
Balanced Hybrid Fund	Minimum 40% to 60%	Maintains a balanced allocation between equity and debt; aims for moderate growth with relatively lower risk
Conservative Hybrid Fund	20% to 35% equity, 65% to 80% debt	Prioritizes stability and regular income through higher debt exposure; suitable for conservative investors
Dynamic Asset Allocation/ Balanced Advantage Fund	Varies dynamically based on market conditions	Actively adjusts the equity-debt mix to optimize returns and manage risk according to market trends

Hybrid Fund Category	Minimum Investment	Description
Equity Savings Fund	Minimum 65% in equity and equity-related instruments	Minimum 65% in equity and equity-related instruments
Multi Asset Allocation Fund	Minimum 10% in each of three asset classes	Diversifies across multiple asset classes (equity, debt, gold, real estate, etc.) for better risk management

💎 **"Your ₹500 can spark a wealth revolution"**

🌟 *Fact: You can start investing in mutual funds with as little as ₹100* 💸 *Mutual funds make investing accessible for everyone—whether you're a student, a professional, or a retiree. Systematic Investment Plans (SIPs) allow you to invest small amounts regularly, helping you build wealth over time with the power of compounding.* 📊 ✨

💡 *Bonus Tip: SIPs also reduce the impact of market volatility through rupee cost averaging, ensuring you buy more units when prices are low and fewer when they're high.* 🛡️ 📊

Ready to take control of your financial future?

Start investing today—because even the biggest dreams start small. 🏆 ✨

INDEX FUNDS

- Definition: Replicate the performance of a specific market index (e.g., Nifty 50, Sensex).

- Risk Level: Moderate
- Suitable For: Passive investors seeking market returns

EXCHANGE-TRADED FUNDS (ETFS)

- Definition: Similar to index funds but traded on stock exchanges like individual stocks.

- Risk Level: Moderate
- Suitable For: Investors seeking liquidity and transparency

Pro Tip: ETFs are great for those who like real-time control, while index funds are ideal for a hands-off approach. Combine both in your portfolio for flexibility and diversification 💎 ✦

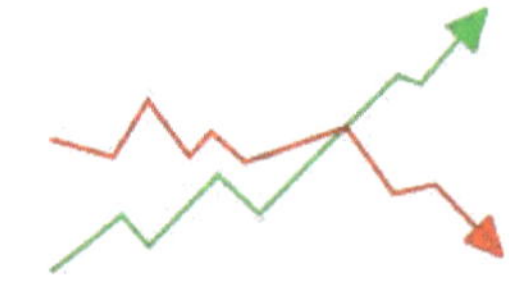

GOLD EXCHANGE TRADED FUNDS (GOLD ETFS)

- Definition: Gold ETFs are mutual fund schemes that invest in gold and gold-related instruments. These funds aim to replicate the performance of gold in the market and are traded on stock exchanges like regular shares.

- Risk Level: Low to Moderate
- Suitable For: Investors looking to invest in gold without the hassles of physical storage.

INTERNATIONAL FUNDS

- Definition: International funds invest in companies and assets located outside the investor's home country. These funds offer exposure to global markets, to diversify their portfolios beyond domestic boundaries.

- Risk Level: High
- Suitable For: Investors seeking diversification and exposure to global market opportunities

ARBITRAGE FUNDS

- Definition: Arbitrage funds exploit price differences between cash and derivatives markets to generate risk-free returns by investing in equity and equity derivatives.

- Risk Level: Low

- Suitable For: Conservative investors seeking low-risk returns with equity taxation benefits.

EQUITY LINKED SAVINGS SCHEME (ELSS)

- Definition: A tax-saving mutual fund with a lock-in period of 3 years.

- Tax Benefit: Eligible for deduction under Section 80C of the Income Tax Act

- Risk Level: High

- Suitable For: Investors seeking tax benefits.

Did you know? ELSS is a fast-growing tax-saving option in India, offering higher returns than traditional instruments ◈ ✦

GOAL-BASED PLANNING IN MUTUAL FUND INVESTMENT

Goal-based planning is a simple yet powerful approach that helps you invest with a clear purpose. Instead of just putting money into mutual funds without direction, this method ensures that your investments align with specific financial goals. Having well-defined goals can make your investment journey more structured and effective.

WHY IS GOAL-BASED PLANNING IMPORTANT?

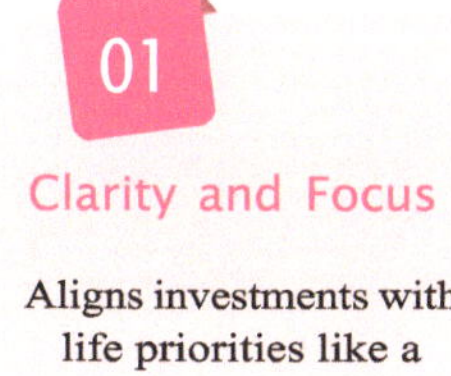

01 Clarity and Focus

Aligns investments with life priorities like a home or retirement.

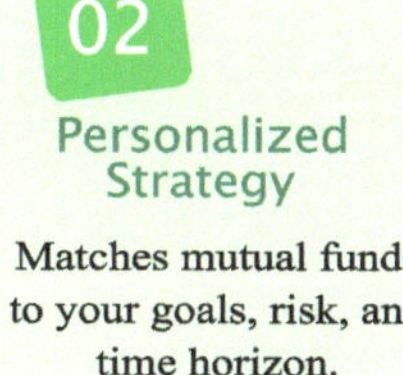

02 Personalized Strategy

Matches mutual funds to your goals, risk, and time horizon.

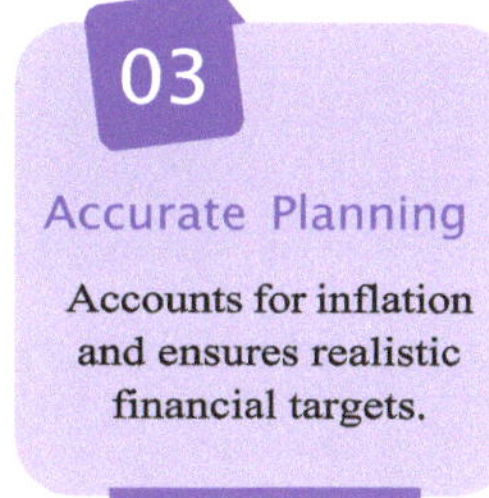

03 Accurate Planning

Accounts for inflation and ensures realistic financial targets.

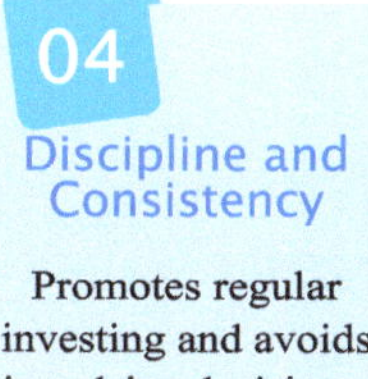

04 Discipline and Consistency

Promotes regular investing and avoids impulsive decisions.

05 Less Emotional Decisions

Keeps focus on long-term goals during market volatility.

06 Goal-Based Success

Tracks progress by goal achievement, not market returns.

INTRODUCTION TO CATEGORIZING FUNDS

Goal planning helps investors prioritize their objectives and select funds based on the time horizon and risk appetite. Broadly, financial goals can be categorized into three types based on their time horizon: short-term, medium-term, and long-term goals. Each category serves different objectives and demands a specific approach to investing.

SHORT-TERM GOALS

Time Horizon: Less than 3 years

Objective: Short-term goals focus on immediate or near-future financial needs where capital protection and liquidity are key. Examples include building an emergency fund, planning a vacation, or saving for a small purchase like a gadget or home appliances.

Recommended Mutual Funds:

- Liquid Funds: Provide high liquidity and minimal risk. Ideal for parking surplus funds for a few months to a year.

- Ultra-Short Duration Funds: Suitable for slightly longer durations, offering better returns than savings accounts while maintaining low risk.

- Debt Funds: Prioritize safety and stable returns over high risk.

Why These Funds?

Short-term goals require investments in instruments that offer safety, stability, and ease of withdrawal to avoid market volatility risks.

Life Happens – Are You Prepared for It?

Imagine this: your car breaks down unexpectedly, a medical emergency arises, or you face a sudden job loss. These are situations that no one plans for but can happen to anyone. The question is, do you have the financial safety net to handle them without falling into debt? That's where an emergency fund becomes your financial superhero!

Emergency Fund

An emergency fund is your financial cushion for life's uncertainties. It's a dedicated pool of money set aside to cover unexpected expenses or financial setbacks, ensuring that your long-term goals remain untouched and your peace of mind intact.

01

How to Start Building Your Emergency Fund

02

Calculate your monthly expenses, multiply by 3-6 months

03

Start small with SIPs to build steadily.

Yes it is essential

- **Security:** Avoids debt during emergencies.

- **Liquidity:** Quick access to money.

- **Peace:** Reduces financial stress.

Take the First Step Today 🚀

Building an emergency fund isn't just smart financial planning—it's a gift 🎁 to yourself and your loved ones. It gives you the confidence 💪 to tackle life's uncertainties while staying on track to achieve your long-term goals.

Start now! 💧 With small, consistent contributions, you'll soon have a financial cushion 🛡 that keeps you secure no matter what life throws your way. Your future self will thank you 🙌 for it.

Time Horizon: 3 to 7 years

Objective: Medium-term goals often involve saving for milestones such as funding higher education, purchasing a car, or planning for a wedding. Here, investors seek a balance between risk and return.

Recommended Mutual Funds:

- Balanced Hybrid Funds: Combine equity and debt to offer moderate growth and reduced volatility.

- Short-to-Medium Duration Debt Funds: For conservative investors aiming for predictable returns over the medium term.

- Aggressive Hybrid Funds: For those willing to take moderate risks, as they invest a higher portion in equities.

Why These Funds?

Medium-term goals demand a blend of growth and stability, with moderate risk to maximize returns without being overly exposed to market volatility.

Invest in Your Child's Dreams – Plan for Their Education Today 🎓

Every Parent's Aspiration

As parents, you want the best for your child—especially when it comes to their education. Whether it's funding their higher studies in India or sending them abroad, quality education opens doors to a brighter future, be prepared to support your child's aspirations without compromising your own goals?

Why Start a Child Education Fund?

Rising Costs : Education expenses grow 8-10% annually; ₹10 lakh today could be ₹20 lakh in 5-7 years.

Avoid Stress: Plan early to avoid high-interest loans or financial strain.

Secure Dreams : Ensure your child's aspirations are achieved without hurdles.

A Case Study to Inspire You 📖

Let's say your child is 8 years old, and you expect to need ₹20 lakh for their higher education in 10 years. By investing just ₹8,000 per month in a mutual fund with an average return of 12%, you can comfortably reach your goal without stress (with a 5% step up every year).

How to Plan for Your Child's Education?

PLANNING

SET A TARGET

START EARLY

CHOOSE THE RIGHT FUNDS

❶ Plan for Your Child's Education

❷ Estimate the future cost of your child's education, factoring in inflation and any additional expenses.

❸ The sooner you start, the smaller the monthly contribution needed to reach your goal. Systematic Investment Plans (SIPs) are an excellent way to build the required corpus.

❹
- Balanced Hybrid Funds
- Aggressive Hybrid Funds
- Equity Funds with Medium-Term Focus

Why Mutual Funds Are Perfect for Child Education Goals —   ✕

- Power of Compounding: Investing early allows your money to grow exponentially over time.

- Inflation-Beating Returns: Mutual funds, particularly equity-oriented ones, offer returns that outpace inflation, ensuring you meet rising education costs.

- Flexibility: You can start with small SIPs and increase contributions as your income grows.

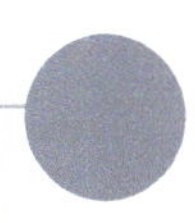

Start now! 🏫 The earlier you begin, the easier it will be to build a robust education fund. Let mutual funds turn your dreams into reality.

CHILD WEDDING

Every parent dreams of giving their child a memorable wedding. Whether it's a grand celebration or an intimate gathering, weddings come with significant expenses. The question is—are you financially prepared to fulfill this dream without disrupting your other financial goals?

Why Plan for Your Child's Wedding Early?

- Rising Costs 💰 – Wedding expenses grow 8-12% yearly; ₹10 lakh today may be ₹25 lakh in 10 years.

- Avoid Stress 😰 – Early planning prevents loans, savings withdrawals, and financial strain.

- Make It Special 💝 – A dedicated fund ensures a dream

Example to Inspire You 📖

If you plan a wedding budget of ₹20 lakh in 10 years, investing just ₹7,000 per month in a mutual fund with 12% annual returns can help you reach your goal stress-free (with a 5% step up every year).

How to Build a Child Wedding Fund?

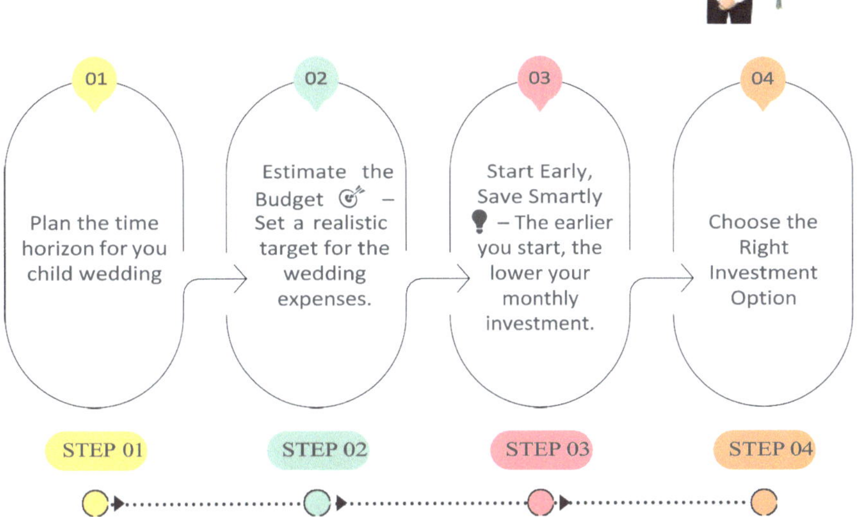

LONG-TERM GOALS

Time Horizon: More than 7 years

Objective: Long-term goals typically include wealth creation, retirement planning, or purchasing a home. These goals allow investors to take higher risks for potentially higher returns due to the power of compounding and the ability to ride out market volatility.

Recommended Mutual Funds:

- Equity Funds: Focused on capital appreciation, equity funds are ideal for wealth creation over the long term. Categories like large-cap, mid-cap, and small-cap funds cater to varying risk appetites.

- Index Funds: Passive funds that replicate market indices, offering long-term growth at a lower cost.

- ELSS (Equity Linked Savings Scheme): Suitable for long-term wealth creation with the added benefit of tax savings.

Why These Funds?

Long-term goals provide the flexibility to embrace higher risks for greater potential rewards, leveraging equity's ability to outperform other asset classes over extended periods.

Turn Your Dream Home into Reality – Start Investing Today 🏡 ✦

Owning a dream home is more than just an investment it's a milestone, a place where memories are built, and security is ensured for your family. But with rising property prices, are you financially prepared to buy your dream home without burdening yourself with excessive loans?

Why Plan for Your Dream Home Early?

- Rising Prices – Real estate grows 7-10% yearly, making homes costlier over time.

- Lower Loan Burden – A planned fund reduces or avoids heavy home loans.

- Own Sooner – Systematic investing helps buy your home faster without financial strain.

Example to Inspire You 📖
If your dream home costs ₹1 crore in 15 years, investing ₹15,000 per month in a mutual fund with 12% annual returns can help you achieve your goal stress-free (with a 5% step up every year).

How to Build a Dream Home Fund?

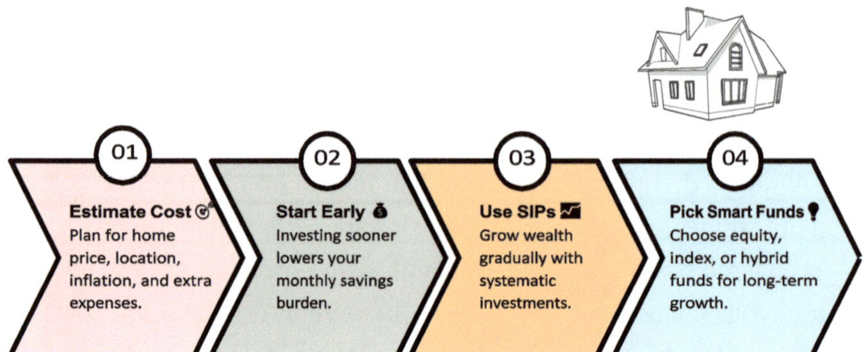

"Buy your dream home with confidence, not loans—invest wisely, start early 🏠 💰 *"*

Start Your Journey Today 🚀

Your dream home is within reach— don't wait for the right time, create the right time! Invest smartly today and turn your vision into reality. 🏠 🔑

Retire Rich, Live Free – Start Your Retirement Plan Today ✦

Retirement isn't just about stopping work—it's about having the freedom to enjoy life on your own terms. Whether it's traveling the world, pursuing your passions, or simply living stress-free, a well-planned retirement fund ensures you never have to depend on anyone financially. But are you preparing for it the right way?

Why Start a Retirement Fund Early?

- Rising Cost of Living 📊 – Inflation erodes purchasing power. What costs ₹50,000 per month today may require ₹1.5 lakh in 20 years.

- No More Monthly Salary 💼 – Your retirement fund replaces your paycheck, ensuring financial independence.

- Longer Life Expectancy ⧖ – With people living longer, a well-planned fund ensures you don't outlive your savings.

- More Time = More Wealth 💰 – The earlier you start, the more you benefit from compounding and lower investment requirements.

How to Build a Strong Retirement Fund?

Set a Target 🎯

Estimate your retirement expenses, including healthcare, lifestyle, and inflation.

01

02

Start Early, Invest Consistently 

SIPs in mutual funds allow small, regular contributions to build wealth.

Choose the Right Investments

- Equity Funds
- Hybrid Funds
- Retirement-Specific Funds

03

Secure Your Golden Years Now! 🚀

Retirement is a journey you should enjoy, not worry about. Start investing today and build a retirement fund that lets you live life on your own terms! ✽

Example to Inspire You 📖

If you need ₹3 crore for retirement in 25 years, investing ₹10,000 per month in a mutual fund with 12% returns can help you reach this goal stress-free.

WEALTH CREATION

Wealth creation is not just about earning—it's about growing your money strategically to achieve financial freedom.

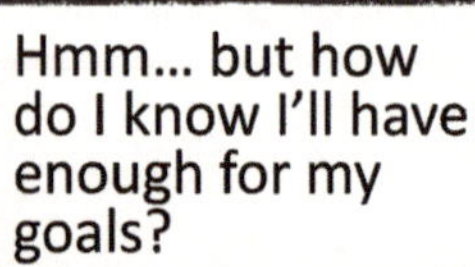

That sounds great, but what if the market fluctuates?

That's the beauty of long-term investing! Over time, equity mutual funds have consistently outperformed inflation and other savings options. The key is to stay invested and let your money grow.

Hmm... but how do I know I'll have enough for my goals?

It's all about planning smartly. Let's say you invest just ₹10,000 per month in a mutual fund with 12% annual returns. In 25 years, that could grow to ₹3.5 crore, with a 10% step up every year! Imagine the financial freedom that brings!

Wow! That's a huge amount! But what if I don't have ₹10,000 to start?

No problem at all! You can start with as little as ₹500 per month through SIPs and increase it as your income grows. What matters is getting started early! Time, not timing, is what builds real wealth.

Start Your Wealth Journey Now 

Wealth isn't just about money—it's about freedom, security, and a life without financial worries. Take the first step today and watch your wealth grow!

Pro Tip for Wealth Creation 💡

"The key to wealth isn't timing the market, but time in the market"

⏳ 📈 *Start investing early, stay consistent with SIPs, and let compounding work its magic. Even small investments grow into huge wealth over time* 🚀 💰

MODES OF INVESTING IN MUTUAL FUNDS

There are three main ways to invest in mutual funds and grow your wealth . Each method has its own benefits depending on your financial goals and risk appetite.

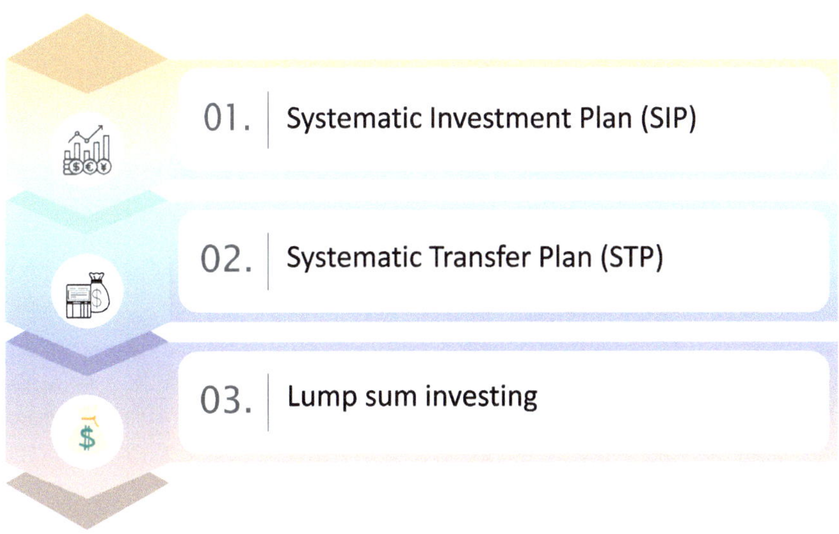

SIP vs. Lumpsum: If you invest ₹1.2 lakh in a lumpsum or ₹10,000 per month via SIP for a year in an equity mutual fund with 12% annual returns, after 10 years, the SIP investment can outperform lumpsum due to rupee cost averaging!

Moral? Consistent investing (SIP) often beats timing the market

A Systematic Investment Plan (SIP) is a disciplined investment strategy offered by mutual funds that allows investors to contribute a fixed amount of money at regular intervals typically monthly or quarterly rather than making a lump-sum investment. This approach is designed to help individuals build wealth over time while managing market volatility.

Key features of Systematic Investment Plan (SIP)

Regular Investments

Investors can choose to invest a predetermined amount regularly, which helps in budgeting and financial planning.

Rupee Cost Averaging

SIPs leverage the principle of dollar-cost averaging, where investors buy more units when prices are low and fewer units when prices are high. This averaging effect can lower the overall cost per unit over time, reducing the impact of market volatility.

Compounding Benefits

By investing consistently over a long period, investors benefit from compounding, where returns on investments generate additional earnings. This can significantly enhance the total corpus accumulated at the end of the investment period.

Flexibility

SIPs offer flexibility in terms of investment amounts and intervals. Investors can increase or decrease their SIP amounts or even pause their investments if necessary.

Convenience

SIPs are easy to set up, often requiring just a one-time instruction to debit the specified amount from the investor's bank account at regular intervals. This automated process eliminates the need for manual transactions.

Achieve Financial Goals

An SIP is a smart tool that helps break your big goals into small amount. Just ascertain the investment amount & start investing regularly through an SIP to achieve your dreams.

SIP: POWER OF COMPOUNDING

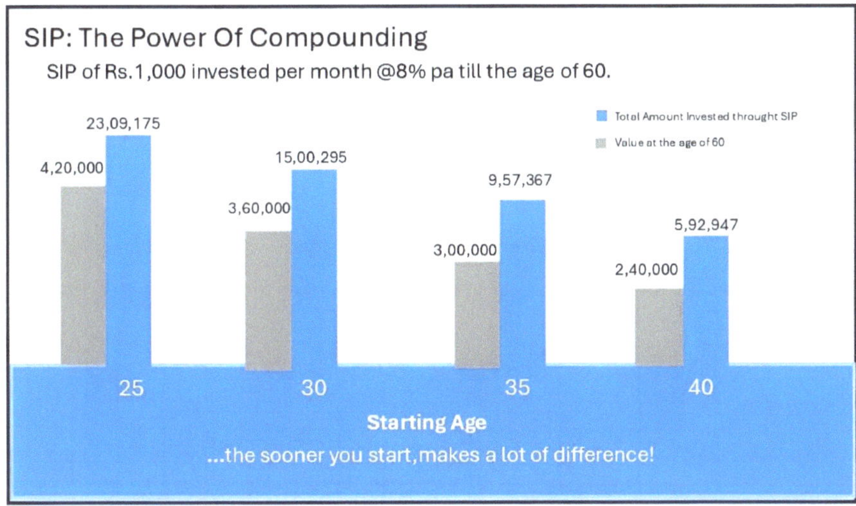

SIP: RUPEE COST AVERAGING

Month	Amount	Rising Market		Falling Market		Volatile Market	
		NAV (Rs)	Units Allotted	NAV (Rs)	Units Allotted	NAV (Rs)	Units Allotted
1	10,000	10	1000	10	1000	10	1000
2	10,000	10.5	952.38	9.5	1052.63	10.5	952.38
3	10,000	11	909.09	9	1111.11	9.75	1025.64
4	10,000	11.5	869.57	8.5	1176.47	10.25	975.61
5	10,000	12	833.33	8	1250.00	12	833.33
6	10,000	12.5	800.00	7.5	1333.33	11.25	888.89
Total	60,000	67.5	5364.37	52.5	6923.55	63.75	5675.85
Avg. Purchase NAV		11.25		8.75		10.63	
Avg. cost per unit		11.18		8.67		10.57	

Life is a roller coaster ride........

Full of ups and downs. We all know we have to save for many responsibilities life bring along with it. But no matter how much you save

IT'S NEVER ENOUGH !!!

SYSTEMATIC TRANSFER PLAN (STP)

A Systematic Transfer Plan (STP) is an investment strategy that allows investors to transfer a fixed amount of money periodically from one mutual fund scheme to another within the same Asset Management Company (AMC). This approach is particularly useful for managing risk and optimizing returns by strategically shifting investments between different types of funds, such as moving from a conservative debt fund to a more aggressive equity fund.

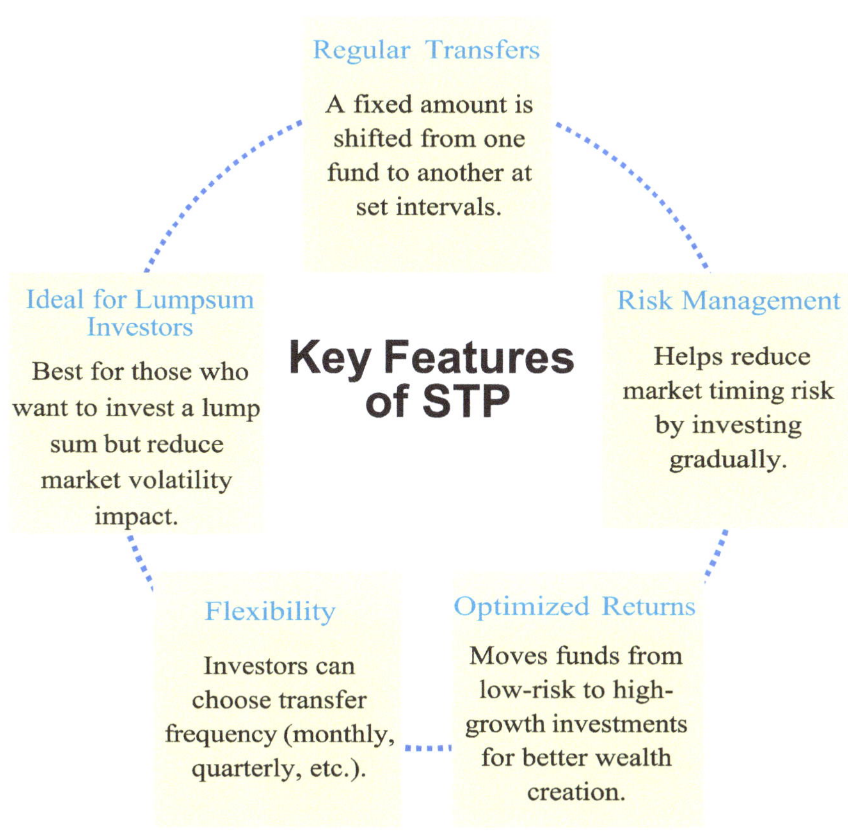

STP is a smart strategy for investors looking to balance stability and growth efficiently. 🚀

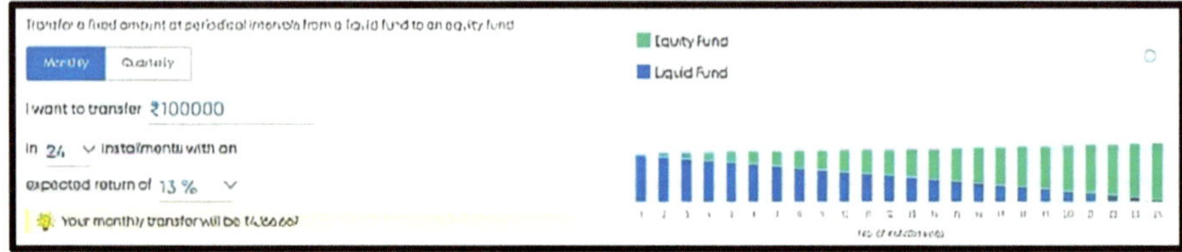

Your Systematic Transfer Plan			
Amount after Transfer	Returns from Liquid Fund	Returns from Equity Fund	Annualised returns
₹1,20,956.219	₹6,219.665	₹14,736.554	10.478%

Value of investment post transfer

₹ 1,20,956.219

Interesting Fact About STP   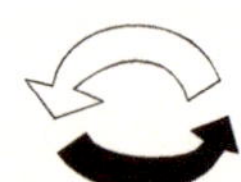

STP acts like a bridge between safety and growth—by moving money from low-risk debt funds to high-growth equity funds, it helps reduce market timing risks while keeping your investments working for you!

Bonus? You earn returns on both sides—steady returns from debt funds while your money gradually enters equities for long-term growth 🚀 🗓️

LUMPSUM INVESTMENT

A Lumpsum Investment means investing a large amount at once in a mutual fund, rather than making small periodic investments like SIP. This strategy is best for investors with surplus funds who want to stay invested for the long term.

1

ONE-TIME INVESTMENT
Invest a bulk amount in one go instead of monthly contributions.

2

HIGHER GROWTH POTENTIAL
Longer market exposure can lead to higher returns over time.

Key Features of Lumpsum

3

MARKET TIMING RISK
Returns depend on when you enter the market; investing at market highs may impact growth.

4

COMPOUNDING BENEFITS
The invested amount grows exponentially over time if left untouched.

5

SUITABLE FOR LONG-TERM INVESTORS
Best for those with a high-risk appetite and long-term financial goals.

Lumpsum Investment Fact 💡

Invest ₹10 lakh in an equity fund at 12% annual returns, and in 20 years, it can grow to 96 Lakhs+ 🚀

Lesson? Lumpsum works best for long-term growth. 📊 💰

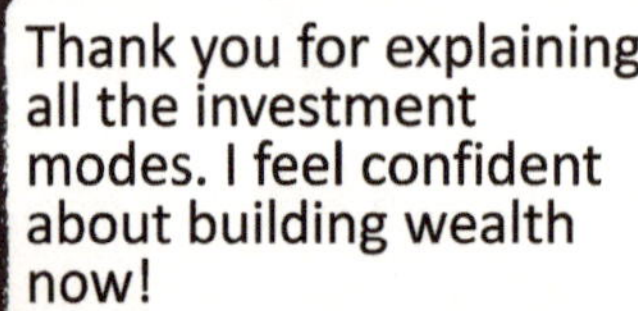

Thank you for explaining all the investment modes. I feel confident about building wealth now!

That's great! Investing is the first step, and staying invested is key to long-term wealth creation.

Now, once I've built a good corpus, how do I withdraw my money?

You have three options:
Full Withdrawal
Partial Withdrawal
SWP (Systematic Withdrawal Plan)

SWP sounds interesting! Can you explain it clearly?

Sure! i will explain you all the three options is detail.

MAKE MONEY
WORK FOR YOU

A full withdrawal means redeeming your entire mutual fund investment at once. This is useful when you need a large sum of money for major expenses like buying a house, a child's wedding, or emergency needs.

Case Study

Rahul invested ₹10 lakh in an equity mutual fund 15 years ago. His investment has grown to ₹54.73 lakh. He decides to withdraw the entire amount to buy a property. However, he faces a capital gains tax on the withdrawn amount, affecting his total returns.

◇ Key Takeaway: Full withdrawal provides instant liquidity, but it may attract taxes and disrupt future wealth growth.

PARTIAL WITHDRAWAL – TAKING OUT ONLY WHAT YOU NEED

Partial withdrawal allows you to redeem a portion of your investment while keeping the rest invested. This ensures that your remaining amount continues to grow.

Case Study

Meera had invested ₹5 lakh in a hybrid mutual fund, and it has now grown to ₹12 lakh. She needs ₹2 lakh for her child's education but doesn't want to disturb the entire investment. She withdraws ₹2 lakh and lets the remaining ₹10 lakh continue growing.

◇ Key Takeaway: Partial withdrawal provides flexibility you withdraw only what you need while keeping your investments intact for further growth.

A Systematic Withdrawal Plan (SWP) allows investors to withdraw a fixed amount from their mutual fund investment at regular intervals. It provides steady cash flow while keeping the remaining amount invested for growth.

Key Features of SWP

1 REGULAR WITHDRAWALS

Investors can withdraw a fixed amount monthly, quarterly, or annually.

2 STEADY INCOME

Ideal for retirees or those needing periodic income from investments.

3 CAPITAL PRESERVATION

Only a portion is withdrawn, while the remaining continues to grow.

4 FLEXIBILITY

Investors can adjust withdrawal amounts or stop SWP anytime.

CALCULATION OF SWP - EXAMPLE

By end of the year	Amount Invested	Withdrawn Amount	Returns from your investment	Resultant Amount
2025	₹10,00,000	₹60,000	₹77,831	₹10,17,831
2026	₹10,17,831	₹60,000	₹1,57,088	₹10,37,088
2027	₹10,37,088	₹60,000	₹2,37,885	₹10,57,885
2028	₹10,57,885	₹60,000	₹3,20,347	₹10,80,347
2029	₹10,80,347	₹60,000	₹4,04,605	₹11,04,605
2030	₹11,04,605	₹60,000	₹4,90,804	₹11,30,804
2031	₹11,30,804	₹60,000	₹5,79,099	₹11,59,099
2032	₹11,59,099	₹60,000	₹6,69,657	₹11,89,657
2033	₹11,89,657	₹60,000	₹7,62,660	₹12,22,660
2034	₹12,22,660	₹60,000	₹8,58,304	₹12,58,304
TOTAL		₹6,00,000		

Invested Amount - ₹10,00,000
Withdrawal Monthly - ₹5,000
Time period - 10 years Expected
Return - 8% P.A

AT THE END OF 10 YEARS

Invested Amount - ₹10,00,000

Withdrawn Amount - ₹6,00,000

Returns from your investment
-₹8,58,304 Balance Value - ₹12,58,304

Direct Plan

In a direct plan, investors invest directly with the fund house without involving any distributor or intermediary. As a result, these plans come with a lower expense ratio since there are no commission or distribution costs, making them a cost-effective option.

Regular Plan

A regular plan is invested through an authorized distributor or agent, who earns a commission for their services. Many new investors struggle to choose the right fund, so seeking guidance from a knowledgeable advisor can help them make informed decisions. Even experienced investors may find it challenging to track their portfolio due to time constraints. A financial advisor plays a crucial role in monitoring, reviewing, and rebalancing investments, ensuring that investors stay on track and maximize their returns without unnecessary risks.

<h1 style="text-align:center">CASE STUDY - I</h1>

From Small Beginnings to Big Returns – The Journey with Nippon India Growth Fund

Background

Ramesh, a 35-year-old teacher from Pune, started investing in the Nippon India Growth Fund in January 2018. As someone with a limited understanding of mutual funds, Ramesh chose advisor's help for the fund for its focus on mid-cap stocks, aiming for higher long-term growth.

Investor Profile

- Occupation: Teacher

- Investment Strategy: Monthly SIP of ₹5,000

- Goal: Build a corpus for his child's higher education in 10 years.

Why Nippon India Growth Fund?

The Nippon India Growth Fund is known for its consistent performance in the mid-cap space. Ramesh was advised by his financial planner to start small but stay committed to investing regularly.

Investment Journey

Phase 1: Early Days (2018-2019):
Ramesh invested ₹5,000 every month,
steadily accumulating units. During this time,
mid-cap stocks experienced volatility, but he stuck to his SIP plan,
trusting the fund's long-term potential.

Phase 2: Market Rally (2020-2021):

As mid-cap stocks began to perform well, the fund delivered impressive returns. By mid-2021, the NAV had significantly appreciated, boosting Ramesh's investment value.

Phase 3: Portfolio Rebalancing (2022-2023):

In consultation with his advisor, Ramesh started monitoring his portfolio. He continued his SIPs but decided to redeem a small portion of his gains for diversification into a balanced fund.

Investment Performance

- Investment Period: January 2018 – December 2023 (72 months)

- Total Amount Invested: ₹3,60,000 (₹5,000 x 72 months)

- NAV Growth:

  - NAV in January 2018: ₹50

  - NAV in December 2023: ₹125

- Units Accumulated: ~5,400 units

- Total Value of Investment (as of December 2023): ₹6,75,000

Key Takeaways

- Compounding in Action: Ramesh doubled his money in 6 years due to the power of compounding and disciplined SIP investments.

- Staying Invested Pays: Despite market ups and downs, staying invested in the mid-cap category yielded significant returns over the long term.

- Importance of Rebalancing: Redeeming part of the gains and rebalancing the portfolio ensured Ramesh could protect his profits and reduce risk.

- Fund Selection Matters: The Nippon India Growth Fund's track record of capitalizing on mid-cap growth opportunities was key to Ramesh's success.

Conclusion

Ramesh's journey with the Nippon India Growth Fund highlights how disciplined investing, coupled with sound financial advice, can help achieve life goals. His story serves as inspiration for those hesitant to start small—every big return starts with a small step.

CASE STUDY - II

The Power of SIPs During Market Volatility.

Background

In early 2020, global financial markets faced significant turmoil due

to the COVID-19 pandemic. Many investors, driven by fear, withdrew their investments, incurring losses. However, disciplined investors who continued their SIPs reaped substantial benefits as markets rebounded.

Investor Profile

Sita , a 30-year-old IT professional from Chennai. In January 2020, she began investing ₹10,000 monthly in the SBI Bluechip Fund through an SIP. Despite market fluctuations, Sita remained committed to her investment strategy.

Market Conditions

- March 2020: The market experienced a sharp decline due to pandemic-induced uncertainties.

- Subsequent Period: Markets gradually recovered, reaching new highs by 2023.

Investment Performance

- Total Investment Period: January 2020 to December 2023 (48 months).

- Total Amount Invested: ₹4,80,000 (₹10,000 x 48 months).

As of December 31, 2023, the Net Asset Value (NAV) of the SBI Bluechip Fund was ₹87.20.

To calculate the value of Sita's investment, we need to consider the NAV at each SIP installment. However, for simplicity, we'll use the average NAV over the investment period. Assuming an average NAV of ₹70 (considering the market dip and recovery), Sita would have accumulated approximately 6,857 units.

Estimated Investment Value as of December 31, 2023: ₹5,98,000 (6,857 units x ₹87.20 NAV).

Approximate Gain: ₹1,18,000, representing a return of about 24.6% over four years.

Key Lessons

- Rupee Cost Averaging: SIPs allow investors to purchase more units when prices are low and fewer units when prices are high, averaging out the purchase cost.

- Discipline Over Emotion: Staying invested during market downturns can lead to significant gains when markets recover.

- Long-Term Wealth Creation: Consistent investing, regardless of market conditions, is a proven strategy for building wealth over time.

Conclusion

Sita's experience underscores the importance of maintaining investment discipline through SIPs, even during periods of market volatility. Her commitment not only safeguarded her investments but also yielded substantial returns, highlighting the effectiveness of SIPs in mutual funds like the SBI Bluechip Fund.

Note: The figures above are estimates for illustrative purposes. Actual investment values may vary based on exact NAVs at each SIP installment and prevailing market conditions. Investors should consult financial advisors for personalized advice.

ROLE OF MUTUAL FUND DISTRIBUTOR

Mutual Fund Distributors play a pivotal role in helping individuals achieve financial security and growth. By providing professional advice, simplifying complex processes, and maintaining a strong ethical approach, MFDs ensure mutual funds are accessible to all segments of society, fostering financial inclusion. In other words a Mutual Fund Distributor (MFD) serves as a bridge between mutual fund houses and investors, helping individuals make informed investment decisions while guiding them toward achieving their financial goals.

Fact About Mutual Fund Distributors 

Did you know? A Mutual Fund Distributor (MFD) doesn't just sell funds— they act as a financial guide, helping investors navigate market ups and downs while ensuring their investments align with life goals.

Bonus: MFDs earn through commissions, meaning their success is directly tied to helping clients grow their wealth.

Eligibility to Become a Mutual Fund Distributor

To become a Mutual Fund Distributor, the following qualifications are essential:

1. AMFI Certification:

- The Association of Mutual Funds in India (AMFI) offers a certification program that ensures distributors possess adequate knowledge about mutual funds, their products, and industry regulations.

- Candidates must pass the NISM-Series V-A: Mutual Fund Distributors Certification Exam, conducted by the National Institute of Securities Markets (NISM).

2. SEBI Registration:

- After obtaining the AMFI certification, the individual must register with SEBI (Securities and Exchange Board of India) as a distributor. SEBI ensures compliance with ethical practices and maintains investor protection standards.

3. Know Your Customer (KYC) Compliance:

- Distributors must complete their KYC registration with the relevant authorities.

Responsibilities of a Mutual Fund Distributor

- Educating Clients – Create awareness about mutual funds, types, benefits, and risks. Simplify concepts like diversification, SIP, and NAV for better understanding.

- Understanding Client Needs – Assess risk appetite (high, moderate, low), financial goals (retirement, education, wealth creation), and investment horizon.

- Recommending Suitable Funds – Suggest the right mutual fund schemes (equity, debt, hybrid, ELSS) based on the client's risk profile and goals.

- Portfolio Performance Updates – Provide insights on returns, market trends, and fund manager strategies while helping adjust investments as needed.

- Ongoing Support & Relationship Building – Address investment queries, offer continuous guidance, and build long-term trust with clients

MUTUAL FUND DISTRIBUTOR IN INDIA

- As of February 2024, there are roughly 1.47 lakhs mutual fund distributors (MFDs) in India.

- The mutual fund industry is attracting more distributors due to the improved performance of mutual funds.

- In the insurance industry, there are approximately 24 lakh insurance agents, which represents a small fraction of India's total population of over 140 crore. In comparison, the mutual fund sector has just around 1.5 lakh distributors, an even smaller proportion of the population.So it has a blooming opportunity in future.

MFDs earn through commissions provided by mutual fund houses. These include:

- Trail Commissions: Ongoing fees as long as the investor holds the fund.

How Does an MFD Earn?

As an MFD, your earnings depend on the Assets Under Management (AUM) you accumulate. You earn commissions on the investments made by your clients, and since mutual funds are long-term investments, you keep earning trail commissions every year on the AUM you build!

MFD Earnings Based on AUM

MFDs are categorized into different tiers based on their AUM, with increasing commissions, incentives, and business growth opportunities

However, distributors must prioritize client needs over commissions to build trust and ensure long-term relationships.

Join hands with Ricchie Rich Investments and step into the world of entrepreneurship as a Mutual Fund Distributor (MFD) 💼 ✦

☑ Be Your Own Boss – Create your own business with unlimited earning potential.

☑ Grow with Expert Support – Leverage our expertise, training, and resources to scale your MFD journey.

☑ Transform Lives, Including Yours – Help clients build wealth while securing your own financial future.

◇ "Your Growth, Our Mission – Let's Build Wealth Together" ◇

💡 START TODAY! PARTNER WITH RICCHIE RICH INVESTMENTS AND TURN YOUR AMBITION INTO SUCCESS. 🚀

Take a deep breath and strive for everything from the very beginning.

7-PERSONAL FINANCE RULES

THAT WILL HELP YOU SAVE MONEY

25X INVESTMENT RULE

You can consider retirement when your investments are worth **25 times your annual expenses.**

Ex : If you need **50K** per year, aim for at least **1.25L** in savings

100-AGE RULE

Find out the **percentage of assets** to invest in equities by subtracting your age from **100.**

Ex : If you are **30 years old**, allocate **70% of your assets** to stocks.

50-30-20 RULE

Allocate **50% of income for necessities** (bills, education, food, transport).
Spend 30% on wants (holidays, entertainment, dining).
Save and invest 20% to build wealth.

1ST WEEK RULE

The best wealth-building habit is to **pay yourself first.**

Set aside **10-20% of your income** within the **first week** of each month.

40% EMI RULE

Your total loan repayments should not exceed **40% of your net income.**
Ex : If you earn **10K per month**, keep your mortgage **below 4K.**

6X EMERGENCY FUND

Before investing, ensure you have an **emergency fund** worth **6 times your monthly income.**
Ex : If you earn **6K per month**, maintain an emergency reserve of **36K.**

RULE OF 72

Determine how long it takes to double your investment by **dividing 72 by your expected return.**
Ex : If your expected return is **6%**, your money will double in **12 years.**

RISK ASSOCIATED IN MUTUAL FUNDS

Every investment comes with some level of risk, and mutual funds are no exception. The risk in mutual funds refers to the possibility that the actual returns from the investment may differ from the expected returns or sometimes lower, sometimes higher.

Common types of risks in mutual funds:

- Market Risk: Losses due to market fluctuations.

- Credit Risk: Risk that bond issuers may default on payments.

- Interest Rate Risk: Change in interest rates may affect bond prices.

- Liquidity Risk: Difficulty in selling the securities when needed.

- Inflation Risk: Erosion of purchasing power due to inflation.

Mutual funds vary in risk depending upon

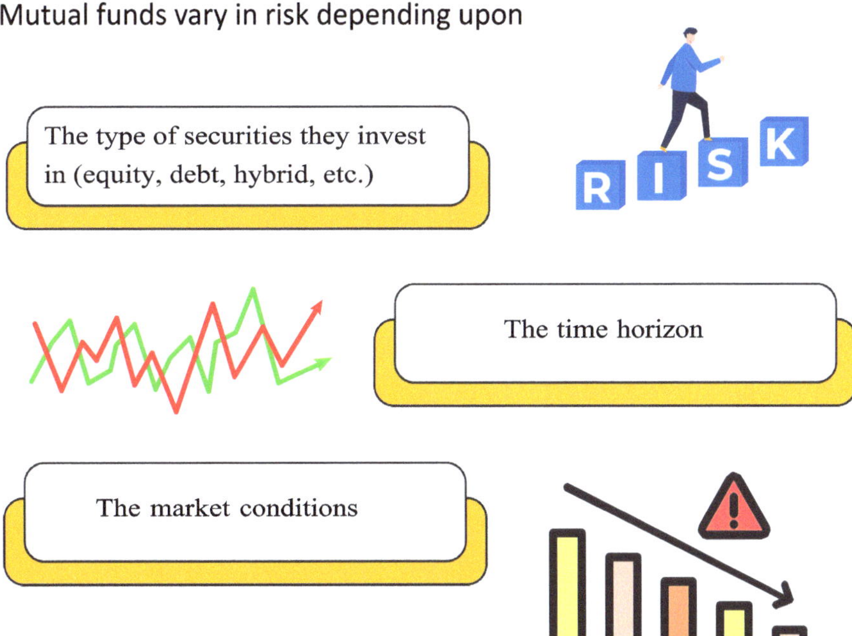

🔨 What is Risk-o-Meter?

Risk-o-Meter is a tool introduced by SEBI (Securities and Exchange Board of India) to help investors easily understand the risk level of a mutual fund scheme. It is represented like a speedometer showing different levels of risk.

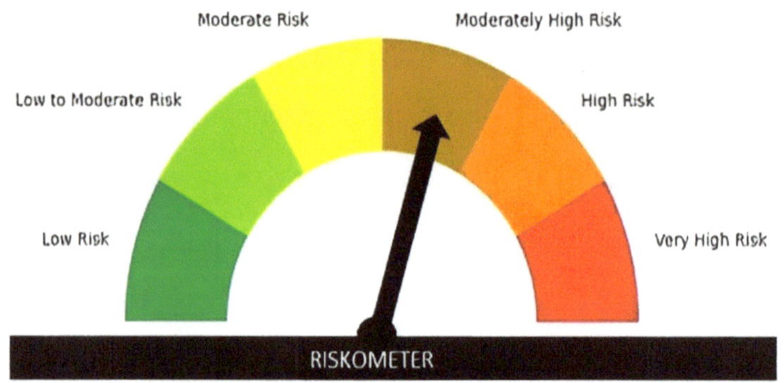

The risk of the scheme/benchmark is [level of risk]

🔨 What Does Risk-o-Meter Say?

- Low (Irish Green) - Very conservative, suitable for risk-averse investors

- Low to Moderate (Chartreuse - Slightly higher returns than low-risk, but still stable

- Moderate (Neon Yellow) - Balanced risk, suitable for moderate investors

- Moderately High (Caramel) - Suitable for investors who can handle market fluctuations

- High (Dark Orange) - Higher return potential but with significant volatility

- Very High (Red) - Aggressive funds for investors with a high-risk appetite

Importance of Risk-o-Meter:

Helps investors match their risk appetite with the fund's risk level.

Ensures transparency from the fund house.

Aids in better goal-based financial planning.

Helps to compare multiple funds quickly through visual.

The Risk-o-Meter gives a visual indication of the risk-return profile of the mutual fund. An investor would be advised to do careful research oneself. In case one is unable to do so, one must consider taking help of a mutual fund distributor or a registered investment advisor.

"Turning Risk into Opportunity: A Case Study on Long-Term Mutual Fund Investing"

Background

Mr. Raj, a 30-year-old investor, started investing ₹5,000 per month in a well-diversified equity mutual fund in 2010. He remained invested till 2024 (14 years).

Risk Faced

Faced market crashes in 2011, 2015, COVID crash in 2020, and market volatility due to global events.

Strategy

- Mr. Raj chose a diversified equity fund instead of sectoral/thematic funds.

- He practiced SIP (Systematic Investment Plan), investing regularly regardless of market highs or lows.

- He didn't panic during market crashes due to a long-term goal.

Outcome

- Despite temporary market falls, the power of diversification and regular investing helped smoothen the volatility.

- His portfolio compounded wealth efficiently over time and beat inflation.

- Risk diversified across multiple sectors, stocks, and market cycles reduced the overall portfolio risk.

CASE STUDY - II

"The Power of Diversification – Rina's Lesson from Sectoral vs Diversified Funds"

Background

Rina, aged 28, invested ₹1,00,000 in 2018 in a Thematic Fund focused on the IT sector, expecting higher returns. At the same time, she also invested ₹1,00,000 in a Diversified Equity Fund.

Risk Faced

- Between 2018 and 2020, the IT sector performed well, and Rina's thematic fund gave good returns.

- However, in 2020-2021, due to regulatory changes and global factors, the IT sector underperformed severely.

- The thematic fund portfolio value dropped by nearly 30%.

- In contrast, the diversified fund, which was spread across multiple sectors (banking, FMCG, pharma, IT, etc.), managed to limit the downside to only 10% loss during the same period.

Outcome

- Thematic and sectoral funds can be high-risk, as they depend on the performance of a single sector.

- Diversified funds reduce sector-specific risk by spreading investments across different sectors.

- Rina realized that for long-term wealth creation, diversified funds provide better risk-adjusted returns than thematic funds.

Both Raj's and Rina's experiences highlight that understanding the Risk-o-Meter and seeking professional advice can help investors align their portfolios with their risk appetite, diversify effectively, and achieve long-term financial goals with confidence.

TAX HARVESTING WITH MUTUAL FUNDS: A SMART WAY TO SAVE CAPITAL GAINS TAX

Most mutual fund investors unknowingly pay more tax than required. One powerful, yet underused, technique is Tax Harvesting a fully legal method to reduce your tax liability by smartly booking losses.

What is Tax Harvesting?

Tax harvesting is the practice of selling loss-making investments to offset capital gains and reduce your tax burden. It helps investors turn paper losses into tax savings while staying invested for long-term goals.

Mutual funds vary in risk depends on

Save capital gains tax legally.

Clean up underperforming funds.

Losses don't go waste they can be used for 8 years.

Boost overall returns by reducing the tax drag.

Capital Gains Tax on Mutual Funds

Type of Capital Gain	Holding Period	Tax Rate
Short-Term Capital Gains (STCG)	< 1 year	20%
Long-Term Capital Gains (LTCG)	> 1 year	12.5%

How Tax Harvesting Works in Mutual Funds

- Identify Loss-Making Mutual Funds - Review your portfolio and spot funds trading below your purchase cost.

- Sell and Book Losses - Sell such funds before 31st March to realize the losses.

- Offset Capital Gains - First, use the loss to offset STCG (higher tax). Remaining losses can offset LTCG beyond the ₹1.25 lakh exemption.

- Carry Forward Losses - Excess losses can be carried forward for up to 8 years to adjust against future capital gains.

- Reinvest Smartly - Invest the proceeds in a similar, but not identical mutual fund to maintain your asset allocation.

Example

Mr. Sharma has ₹2 lakh LTCG from equity mutual funds and ₹70,000 losses from another underperforming mutual fund.

Without Tax Harvesting:

- LTCG tax = 12.5% of (₹2 lakh - ₹1.25 lakh exemption) = ₹9,375

With Tax Harvesting:

- Net LTCG = ₹2 lakh - ₹70,000 = ₹1.3 lakh

- Taxable LTCG = ₹1.30 lakh - ₹1.25 lakh = ₹5,000

- LTCG Tax = ₹625

Tax Saved = ₹8,750 instantly!

Tax Harvesting is a simple, effective, and legal strategy to reduce taxes and enhance long-term returns. Every mutual fund investor should consider this while doing annual portfolio review.

Disclaimer: Investors are advised to consult a qualified Chartered Accountant or tax consultant before implementing this strategy.

STOCK	A share represents ownership in a company, giving you a right to a portion of its profits and assets.
IPO (INITIAL PUBLIC OFFERING)	The first time a company sells its shares to the public, allowing it to raise funds by listing on the stock exchange.
BLUE-CHIP STOCK	Shares of well-established, reputable, and financially stable companies.
PENNY STOCK	Low-priced stocks with small market capitalization that are highly volatile.
BULL MARKET	A market where stock prices are rising, indicating investor confidence and economic growth.
BEAR MARKET	A market where stock prices are falling, signaling economic concerns or a downturn.
DIVIDEND	A part of a company's profits that is shared with its shareholders.
PAYOUT RATIO	The percentage of a company's profits paid to shareholders as dividends.

POWER WORDS FOR MUTUAL FUND 🚀

BONUS SHARES	Extra shares given to existing shareholders for free, increasing the total number of shares they own.
BUYBACK	When a company repurchases its own shares, reducing supply and boosting the value of remaining shares.
STOCK SPLIT	A corporate decision to divide shares, making them more affordable and increasing liquidity.
NAV (Net Asset Value)	The per-unit value of a mutual fund, calculated as (Total Assets - Total Liabilities) / Total Mutual Fund Units.
EXPENSE RATIO	The fee a mutual fund charges for managing investments; a higher ratio reduces returns, and a lower ratio increases them.
NFO (New Fund Offer)	The first-time offer of units in a mutual fund, similar to an IPO in the stock market.
FUND OF FUNDS	A mutual fund that invests in other mutual funds instead of individual stocks or bonds.

LOCK- IN PERIOD	A required holding period before an investor can withdraw from a mutual fund, common in tax-saving schemes.
LIQUID FUND	A mutual fund that invests in short-term debt instruments, providing safety and quick access to funds but with lower returns.
CAPITAL GAIN	Profit earned from selling assets like stocks or mutual funds at a higher price than the purchase cost.
CAPITAL LOSS	Loss incurred when selling assets like stocks or mutual funds for a lower price than the purchase cost.
CAGR (Compound Annual Growth Rate)	The average annual growth rate of an investment over a period, considering compounding.
XIRR (Extended Internal Rate of Return)	A more accurate return calculation for investments with irregular cash flow
ABSOLUTE RETURN	The total percentage gain or loss on an investment over a specific period, without considering time.
AUM (Assets Under Management)	The total value of assets managed by a mutual fund or financial institution.

ROE (Return on Equity)	Measures a company's profitability by showing how much profit is generated per unit of shareholder equity.
ROCE (Return on Capital Employed)	Evaluates how efficiently a company uses its capital to generate profits.
ROA (Return on Assets)	Indicates how efficiently a company uses its assets to generate net profit.
P/E Ratio (Price-to-Earnings Ratio)	Shows how much investors are willing to pay per rupee of earnings; a measure of stock valuation.
CAGR (Compound Annual Growth Rate)	Shows how much investors are willing to pay per rupee of earnings; a measure of stock valuation.
P/B Ratio (Price-to-Book Ratio)	Compares a company's market price to its book value, indicating whether it is over or undervalued.
EPS (Earnings Per Share)	The profit earned per share, calculated as net profit divided by the total number of outstanding shares.

Conclusion

Mutual funds are not just about investing, they are about financial empowerment. With the right planning and discipline, anyone can build wealth and achieve their financial aspirations. Whether you're an investor seeking growth or a distributor looking to create an impact, the journey to financial success starts with knowledge and action.

The key to wealth creation is consistency, patience, and informed decision making. Time in the market is more important that timing the market. Start today! 🚀

Thank you for exploring—invest, grow, succeed! ✦

https://ricchierichinvestments.com